One Day Me Be Fine

Essays and Poems

Susan K. Brown

ISBN: 1500290157
ISBN-13: 978-1500290153

DEDICATION

For
my husband
who walked this
journey with me.

CONTENTS

FORWARD

This is the story of my dear wife's journey toward wholeness and wellness. She writes eloquently about her fears, her terror, her loves, and her tender heart toward others.

She passes over what should be obvious to the casual reader, however. This journey has made us both stronger people.

Better now we understand the plight of the homeless who has the same diagnosis that we received, but who do not have insurance coverage to treat it. Better now we understand the impulse in the Christian church to disregard or dismiss mental health issues. Better now we understand the crisis moment of being called from a classroom by a security office to rush to the local emergency room. Better now we understand how law enforcement, health care providers, and spiritual leaders are prepared, or not, to wrestle with the dread we fought.

Recovery support groups tell their members to cling to the belief in a Higher Power. Our deep faith in Jesus the Christ has kept us moving forward on our journey. While this is Susan's journey, we have made the trip together. I count it a privilege to be her husband.

--Daniel S. Brown, Jr.

ACKNOWLEDGMENTS

I am deeply thankful to the following:

My husband for always being by my side. For his encouragement to write my story. He told me I would know when it was time to write.

My mom and dad who prayed for protection of my life and for healing.

My therapist who early on in my treatment encouraged me to write my story to help others understand mental illness.

My psychiatrist who saw my writing as part of my healing journey.

My family doctor for following my journey and helping to save my life.

HEART SONG: A SONG OF JOY

My heart sings with joy
I know I am a child of the King
I am loved with an everlasting love,
I can bring my most inner thoughts and needs to
    the Lord
He is always present.
I just need to call on His name
He will hear my cry and answer
It is with great delight, honor and praise
That God has delivered me from
The evil thoughts and voices for a season
I give thanks unto the Lord for his miraculous
    work in ME.

1
WASSUP?

Everyone has a story. Some are funny. Some have you bending over laughing so hard you want to cry. Some stories are sad and you hurt for the person that is suffering. Let me tell you a story. My story.

The story is my personal account from almost losing life to finding life again.

> The pain comes from deep within—
> It invades my soul
> It cries out in frightening ways
> Paralyzing my day
> Screaming for help
> Anxiety over small easy tasks,
> That become insurmountable daily obstacles.
> Pleading for death so that all will be peaceful
> My soul cries out for help.
> Who is listening?
> Oh God rescue me from my pain.

My story begins when my family moved from a big Midwest City to a small town in western, Pennsylvania in the summer of 2001. It was a big life event. After a year I began my own piano studio and a year later accepted a position at a local university. My new job was the realization of a goal that I had for many years. I supervised student teachers in the field. I was elated!

While the journey began with the move to a small town and the job at the local university, in the summer of 2007, the journey took a sharp, dark turn. It was a journey where I nearly lost my life.

It was a slow journey of isolating myself and hiding my pain for many months. I didn't share my struggles with anyone until the spring of 2008. By that time I wanted to die. Now I began to feel the pain from deep inside. I screamed out but not audibly.

I continued to teach and work. My journey took me on many paths but daily life was becoming increasingly difficult. I could not rescue "me" from my pain. I found this journey insurmountable. While I experienced many mountain tops where life was good for three to six months at a time, I experienced far more days in a deep, dark valley crying out for someone to listen and rescue me from this pain. I didn't know it would take six long years to experience relief from this unrelenting pain.

I began to make changes in my journey. I tried to save my life. I learned slowly not to share information about what I was experiencing with my family, friends and pastors. They did not understand. Some of their responses would make the top-ten list of things you should never say to a hurting person.

They would just look at me and say, "Everyone has bad days." "Do you think you are demon possessed?" "You have a good life; you have a wonderful husband who loves you and a great job. Tell me why you want to kill yourself." I found these questions and statements obnoxious.

People are so misinformed and trying to provide information to help people understand what I was going through was like trying to put a camel through the eye of a needle.

I am writing about my journey to help people understand mental illness through the eyes of one who is surviving. Through my eyes. I learned that I have schizoaffective disorder. What is that? The way it was explained to me is that I have a light form of schizophrenia and a light form of bipolar depressive. Practically speaking that means I hear voices and see things that aren't actually there. I have sudden mood drops that I find bring me to a place of darkness, sadness, aloneness and abandonment. Sometimes I experience mania; I have too much energy, revved up thinking and a heightened sense of creativity. Wassup? I found a long journey with many twists and turns and mostly with deep dark valleys for years.

There were many days during those years that I would have welcomed death. I struggled to keep my life together. I was barely able to keep my piano studio going and meet with my student teachers.

Hospitalizations were kept secret, but all my students and the university thought I was "out sick." I thought if people knew my situation they would plot against me and keep me from doing the work I loved.

So I stayed in a hideable hell where my pain cried out for peace. I found as the years passed by that daily tasks were so difficult that I just started a spiral where I could no longer do my jobs, do the laundry, clean the house, cook meals, get groceries and enjoy daily life. All I did was teach and I was losing the ability to do that well. I was lost on the journey to save my life.

2
THE SHROUD

The veil covers my entire body.
I can't see out, it is very dark.
I can't feel my face.
There is a dense fog all around me.
I feel cold
I feel dead
I am totally helpless
I can't tear through the shroud
No one can hear my screams
The shroud is always with me

SUSAN K. BROWN

3
MIND WARP

I found myself trapped in my mind.

I heard voices. The voices told me to harm myself. They told *how* to harm myself. I would believe that I should kill myself because the voices told me I had no business being on earth.

I heard voices telling me to "die, bitch die," and many similar commands. I heard voices tell me how to kill myself. The voices told me to kill myself with pills. Now at this point many might think "This is stupid, get your act together and get on with life."

A therapist tried to encourage me by asking, "What would Queen Latifah do?" She would kick these voices' butts.

I couldn't kick butts.

I was trapped with these tricks that my mind played on me and I could not distinguish what was real from what was not real. So, I counted out pills and stared at them for hours trying to get the courage to take them and end the pain deep within my soul.

The voices told me to drown myself in the shower but somehow this option seemed stupid. I couldn't figure out what to do. Phew! At least death-by-showering was off the table.

The other fascination that I had was knives. The voices told me not to slash my wrists but to stab myself. I often held the knives but never acted on using the knife to end my life.

The sad thing is that on numerous occasions I acted on the commands by using pills to silence the voices so that the pain would end. Smart people would say, something like "What is wrong with you?" I didn't see taking pills as being wrong. I was not able to comprehend the truth that the voices were not real. I struggled to stay in the here and now, the present.

My mind played tricks on me that I wasn't able to understand. The voices commanded me to die during worship services at the church. The voices would come through the bass tones in the music. I stopped going to church.

This was my reality. This was my hell. I was not living in the here and now. I was living in a world that my voices and I had created. This was my world of living; taking pills to end the voices.

4
MIND TRICKS

My brain is crashing. I am lost.
I'm being hurt.
I need to cry.
Standing outside of me.
Don't know the end.

SUSAN K. BROWN

5
BOUND

I feel bound up
Struggling to breathe.
Feeling reality slipping away.
Hanging on to familiar things
Trying to stay in the here and now
Counting blessings
So
    I
        Don't
            Slip
                Away

6
FLIPPING OUT

What world am I in?
Heart pounding fast and shaking inside.
I don't know what's happening to me.
I am scared.
I don't want to die.
I'm scared a part of me is slipping away.
I'm dizzy from all of these voices I hear.
I need help. But, not just yet.

7
HOSPITALS ARE LIKE ZOOS

At several different times I found myself trapped in the hospital system.

I remember clearly my first hospitalization. The behavioral health unit was scary. I couldn't get anyone to tell me what was going on with my treatment. My treatment plan was a big mystery and a conspiracy to keep me from getting better. I thought the doctors would try something new and innovative.

The harsh reality was there were no medication changes. I then just sat and waited until my insurance wouldn't pay for any more days, and then I was released back into my life.

I realized hospitals are like zoos. You are caged in a locked unit only to be let out to eat and some places not let out anywhere until you leave. Hospitals are like zoos because they feed you and provide you with a place to sleep, and allow visitors to come and see you.

When the hospital opens the door it is like an animal at a zoo having its cage door opened and I was now vulnerable in the world again. I was back in the real world where everything became a challenge.

I always thought the hospital would make all my symptoms go away. I thought this for a very long time. This was another way that I became trapped. The hospital system was a band aid for a much larger problem for me.

The larger problem came with its own series of questions." How do I stay out of the hospital system?" "How do I hide my symptoms?" "How do I keep people from knowing I just took pills?" Fortunately, I was not good at hiding things.

I felt very frustrated by the hospital system. The doctors kept their distance and had very little interaction with patients during the stay. The hospital system was and is overcrowded. The hospital was and is understaffed. The hospital took at least 24 hours before allowing access to your medicines. These were the medications my doctor, the one who best knew my medical situation had prescribed to keep me alive.

While I did take part in the daily or twice-daily required group sessions I did not find them well organized or helpful when all I wanted to do was kill myself. This was my first hospitalization. Before the journey was over I would be admitted to other hospitals.

The behavioral health units in the four hospital systems that I found myself in had one thing in common: There were many people with worse symptoms than mine and these people were scary. The screaming and crying out I never got used to.

I learned that hospitals were a place where you did your time and waited for your release date. I found myself trapped in the hospital system off and on for six years. When I tried to kill myself or when I said that I would harm myself, I was admitted for the mandatory seven days – longer if the hospital could convince my insurance that I needed an extended stay.

The hospital became a crazy-making place where my entire life would be gone for seven to ten days at a stretch. I was continuing to slip away and losing the battle to stay alive.

8
WARMLY EMBRACED

Wet
Drops
Streaming
Gently down my face
Oh quiet whimpers of despair
Know that I am your God
Look upward and let the light shine upon
My countenance
Be sad no more

SUSAN K. BROWN

9
UNPLUGGED

I found myself trapped by medications. When I took my medications I saw my eyes as hollow and glazed. I did not see me when I looked in a mirror. I saw a human form with hollow eyes. I no longer recognized myself. I was gone.

While the medications were meant to help with my symptoms, they also caused a number of side effects. The ability to concentrate was gone. I couldn't follow conversations which meant I struggled to take part in conversations in small groups where I could interject my thoughts too. I was not able to watch television. The voices were garbled, and I couldn't follow the story line. The medications made me think the television was talking to me. Sometimes the television produced only static white noise. For a long time the television was not played in our home.

Reading was out of the question while on these medications. Whether it was a single medication or the cocktail effect, I did not know.

I had hand tremors so bad that I had to stop playing the piano. I had great difficulty writing and was embarrassed by this because I once had beautiful handwriting. I had taught cursive handwriting in grade school. Now my writing was illegible.

For a long time my anxiety was so high I would wrap myself as tight as I could in a quilt, like a cocoon and stay in that cocoon for hours. I felt numb, unplugged not able to participate in society.

Sometimes my medication combinations worked well together. I loved those times in my journey. I felt vibrant and alive. I was able to do simple daily tasks. I was able to have some conversation and the television was able to be on in the house. Noises did not bother me. I would be able to go out in public and relax. I would actually enjoy myself. Laughter would return to our home. My sense of humor would come back, and I had hope that I was on the healing path of my journey. The problem was that I would relapse, and I felt defeated.

I knew there was another medication change needed and that it would take weeks, maybe months before I would know if the new medicines were going to work. The changes were stressful, and I struggled to be a good patient during these times.

I love books and I have a degree in reading and now I was not able to read anything; not even a magazine article. I saw the medications as a necessary evil to try and bring some sense of normalcy back into my life so that I could be me again.

The medications used to try and save my physical life were killing the real me and I was no longer a vibrant participant in enjoying life. The medications were trapping me and taking away my "me-ness." The me I knew was unplugged from life.

SUSAN K. BROWN

10
WHERE AM I?

I'm in the world but not of the world.
Right now I am not of the world.
I see spirits floating around me.
White wispy blobs with eyes.
Enveloping me. They are after me.
They're trying to catch me.
I can hear their breathing. They are close.
I am running but not fast enough.
They are gaining on me.
I look back. I can see them.
They are going to get me.
No one can protect me.
Walls, Windows, Doors won't stop them,
From finding me.
They aren't from the living world but they look
   real.
I know because I see them.

11
MEMORIES

Puddles
Leaves
Sticks
Beautiful Reflection
A puddle on a trail enveloped in lush green
    grass on each side,
Leaves and sticks under the water
Creating a beautiful montage
The sun is settled in through the trees
There is enough light for a reflective moment.
Longingly wanting to be that transformed
    montage
So as a transformation
    I don't have to question my heart
        As to what I see.

SUSAN K. BROWN

12
BLACK JESUS

On one inpatient experience I met Jesus. Not the real Jesus. This Jesus was a very large African-American woman with a commanding presence. She actually had an entourage of patients that waited on her hand and foot.

She never got her own food in the cafeteria. She always had her own sofa in the patient lounge and you didn't mess with her when it came to two things: First, her naps on the sofa in front of the television that had her favorite show on. Nobody dared change the channel even though she was sleeping. Second, foul language.

She had a way about her and she told it like it was. People always used good, clean language around Jesus. She made people behave, speak and even walk properly. She was the most interesting person that I ever met.

Meeting Jesus in a behavioral health unit was . . . well, crazy.

SUSAN K. BROWN

13
MUSIC AND THE SILENT VOID

Music made me "me." I always had music in my life.

I could hardly wait to get my first piano. I was so ready that I could taste music in my soul. I began studying piano when I was eight years old. I studied sacred and classical piano. At one point I aspired to go to Julliard. Like most kids, my journey took me on a different path. But music always stayed with me.

When I had to close my piano studio after ten years of teaching, I found that was one of the hardest days of my life. From that day forward music became painful. I could no longer play because my hand tremors were so bad that I struggled to make my hands work. When I listened to music it was like nails piercing through my body. The pain was unbearable so music left my life. A silent void took over and I didn't know what to do.

My passion for music is desolate now. The former romance with music now brings pain and sadness. My body screams out in physical and emotional pain at the sound of once beloved pieces.

The joy that music has always played in my life is difficult to understand now. Why is this loss of something once an integral part of my being happening?

My heart breaks for this love that is lost. I know I am on a journey to heal my soul. I need to let my emotional and physical being be comforted by the music that has been my life.

The once-tickled ivories are silent. The piano bench that holds much music never opens now. My hands shake if I sit on the piano bench waiting to play the opening chord, so I just freeze. This is not me, and I don't understand what is happening. I have a deep aching place inside me like a wound that keeps reopening and can't heal.

There is a sense of a great loss of who I am…as though a part of me has been cut off. Where did that part of me go? What does that separation mean? Is that separation the ebb of the tide? Will the flow return? I don't know.

How do I have an affair with music again? I just want to know. I am trying to reach out and grasp onto the hope that my life will once again be filled with music.

What will my renewed passion for music be

like and how long will this renewal take?

I long for this silent part of my "being" to change. I want my "being" that can be soothed in the midst of a stormy day. My "being" that can relax and enjoy the magnificence of Mozart's Concerto in A major for clarinet, Hillary Hans' angelic and soulful violin and the beauty from his soul that Yo-Yo Ma captures on the cello. The soft, relaxing, jazz stylings, of Oscar Peterson. The intense passion of Chico O'farrill as he expresses with intensity the music that he writes and loves. The renderings of Vince Gauraldi that give you an anticipation of what comes next. The sexy voice of Harry Connick Jr. that lets you be swept off your feet by your husband, your lover.

I want music not to hurt anymore. I want that physical pain of music, that pain that crushes my body and feels like nails piercing my skin, to stop. Just stop!

I want romance with music again. I just don't know how to get back to that place of being in touch with my "being" in love with the language and sound of music. I want there to be a grand crescendoing as I search for music to be my "passion," my "being," my "staccato." I just don't know how to start. May this passion return Vivace.

Music was silenced in our house for three years.

SUSAN K. BROWN

14

MUSIC RETURNS ANDANTE

Once in a while during one of my rare manic phases something creative would happen. In 2009 during one of these phases I wrote a song on one of my favorite verses in the Bible. Philippians 4:13. This was an amazing feat that I know was a special gift to help me see that music was returning to my life.

The words to the song:

Rejoice, Rejoice, Rejoice give thanks and sing
Rejoice, Rejoice, Rejoice give thanks and sing
My brothers in Christ rejoice
My sisters in Christ rejoice.

Rejoice, Rejoice, again I say rejoice
Rejoice, Rejoice, again I say rejoice
For I can do all things
For I can do all things, through Christ who
    strengthens me
Through Christ who strengthens me

Be with me when I am in trouble
Be with me when I am in need
Rejoice, Rejoice, again I say rejoice
Rejoice, Rejoice, again I say rejoice
For I can do all things, through Christ who
    strengthens me
Through Christ who strengthens me.

It would be another four years before I realized I was never going to be that great pianist I once was. My romance with music would have a new look. It would be more simple. I returned back to the basics. The place where I first started my love affair with music when I was a child. The part of me that is hope. I began my return by playing the old hymns from my dusty hymnal.

The first song I played had always been a favorite of mine. "How Firm A Foundation," a traditional tune was first published by John Rippon in *Selection of Hymns* in 1787. This song was where I had been on my journey through my mental illness, my fight for finding life again.

How firm a foundation, ye saints of the Lord.
Is laid for your faith in his excellent word!
What more can he say than to you he hath said-
Too you, who for refuge to Jesus have fled.

Fear not, I am with thee – O be not dismayed,
For I am thy God, I will still give thee aid;
I'll strengthen thee, help thee, and cause thee to

stand,
Upheld by my gracious omnipotent hand.

When through deep waters I call thee to go,
The rivers of woe shall not thee overflow;
For I will be with thee thy troubles to bless,
And sanctify to thee thy deepest distress.

When through fiery trials thy pathway shall lie,
My grace, all sufficient, shall be thy supply;
The flame shall not hurt thee – I only design
Thy dross to consume and thy gold to refine.

The soul that on Jesus hath leaned for repose,
I will not I will not desert to his foes;
That soul, tho all hell should endeavor to shake,
I'll never – no, never – no, never forsake!

The words to this song captured where my journey had taken me and I wept as I realized this song brought me back to my love affair with music. After that love returned I practiced eight songs for four months. I performed a mini recital for my husband complete with a brief monologue at the beginning of the recital and refreshments at the end. Music has returned to our home. The music is different. No longer are the days of difficult technical pieces to be played; just simple tunes from an old book, on an old friend, my piano.

SUSAN K. BROWN

15

THE UNSUNG HERO

When you find yourself walking the journey on the path of mental illness you are alone. There are others around you but in your mind you are alone. You are so sick that you don't realize the impact of the illness on those who care about and for you. It is not that you don't care but, try as hard as you can to include that person, you struggle to help him understand the experience.

Without realizing, I slowly stayed in my own world with my voices, the world the voices and I created. It became easier than letting my unsung hero into my inner most dark thoughts. I didn't want to hurt him. In some way I knew that I needed to protect him from the really ugly bad stuff that went on in my mind. In my mind, with my voices. I didn't want to destroy him on this path of my journey. I needed a hero. I needed to be able to look up to someone who was strong. I needed that.

My husband never left my side. He never got angry with me. He was there when I needed to cry and be held in his arms. He carried me through the deep dark valleys when I couldn't walk them alone. He stood with me on the mountain tops. He was there during the times joy and laughter returned to our home and all was going well. He was there when my medicines needed changed, and I felt defeated. He held me close to him and told me it was going to be all right. He believed in me even when I lost all hope for my journey. He was always there.

He loved me and always told me, "I love you." He stood by me. He is my hero.

He always told me from our wedding day forward, "I love you more." I know that he is right.

He is my husband. He is my unsung hero.

16
A SPECIAL FRIEND

There are times in our life when you cultivate a relationship with another person and a friendship blossoms. I have a friend like that. Her name is Sarah. She was and is there for me. She offered and offers to help in a sincere and pure way. She never pushed or pushes me to share but, she listened and listens.

She truly wanted to better understand what I was going through. She wanted to know how she could help. She is a faithful friend.

We saw each other and see each other regularly. One time we had lunch plans. When she came to the house I was sound asleep. My medicines were in the process of being changed, and they made me extremely sleepy. My husband woke me up, and I was startled.

And there was Sarah looking over the love seat at me. She asked if we should go out another day.

"No, I said. "I need to go out today."

"Let's do it."

I rousted and pulled myself together and away we went. I don't recall anything about that lunch except that my friend and I went out to the local coffee shop. It was exactly what I needed.

Over time I continued to heal. Sarah sent me cards, called me, we went out for coffee and lunch and after a long period of time we would go shopping at the local mall. We had a hundred and forty stores to pick from, and we went to our favorite few. We learned that we shopped well together and helped each other not to buy on impulse.

I was happy for a genuine friend who cared deeply for what I was going through. But, more than that I, was happy that she wasn't afraid of my illness. Everyone needs a friend who is always there with you. I needed someone I could share my successes with, my failures, my fears, and just being girls together talking about "girly" things. Sarah cared for me and is a part of my path on my journey to find life again. I love that we are friends.

17
BROKEN FRIENDSHIP

I have a very special friend. My parents introduced me to him when I was very young. We went everywhere together. He grew up with me. He was there when I cried and when I was sad. He was there when I was happy.

Sometimes I would get scared when I struggled in school. A school guidance counselor once told me I would never make it into college. My friend was there as I sobbed uncontrollably. My friend was at my college graduation. He was so happy and pleased with my accomplishment.

My friend was with me as I began my journey into teaching, then into business and back to teaching. We had a great relationship. Sometimes we talked every day. Sometimes my friend and I wouldn't talk for weeks but we always picked up right where we left off.

On my wedding day my friend was there. He

clapped with the guests when the minister introduced us as "Mr. and Mrs. Brown."

When we moved to the South my friend made the move too.

One day my husband and I decided it was time to increase the size of our family. We tried for six months and nothing happened. Nothing. My friend helped me get through the seven years of infertility treatments. He was a good friend. He was their when our hearts ached, when we sobbed, and when we prayed.

My good friend traveled and made the move back to the Midwest with us. This friend meant the world to me.

When I learned I had Schizoaffective disorder, he was there holding my hand. After the diagnosis I would talk to my friend, and he would assure me everything would be all right.

But then something happened to our friendship.

We didn't talk for months at a time. Our friendship became broken. I would ask my friend to sit with me and talk with me, but he was gone. I felt hurt and abandoned and very alone. Our friendship was broken.

I became very angry with my friend. In the fight to save my life he left me to fight alone. I was brokenhearted. I didn't know how to fix my friendship. I was hurting, and he was gone.

My friend was God.

My relationship was broken now. For me and perhaps many others, this is the worst, most menacing part of a mental illness. God is not there.

18
MY LAMP

Oh Lord, why do I feel my lamp is just a
    flicker?
I know I am your child.
I know you are right beside me.
You keep me in your hand at all times-
Please OH, GOD turn my darkness
     into light.

What causes such despondence in my soul?
I ask but you don't answer Lord—
Maybe my mind is too cluttered—
That I don't hear your voice
Help me to be quiet
So I can hear your voice
And turn my darkness into light again.

What keeps my light dark?
A failure to simply recognize the light?
My time needs to include searching for the light,

To keep my lamp burning
A loss of perceived joy that limits my lamp to
    burn.

Loneliness and separation from Yahweh,
Even though he never leaves my side.

A lack of calmness over daily events;
Keeps my lamp darker than it needs to be
Feeling unloved while you love me at
      All Times
So Lord restore my joy, calmness and love—
Remind me you understand me.

19

MENDING A FRIENDSHIP

I was estranged from God.

When I perceived God abandoned me, I was angry and had no desire to have God in my life. I was angry for a very long time. I didn't speak or pray to God. Others prayed for me but I didn't pray.

A long time passed—years—before I even thought about my friendship. I began to wonder if God could forgive me for pushing him out of my life. I began to question if it was okay to be angry with God. As long as we had been friends, I had never been angry at him.

Now I want a relationship again. Now I want to trust God again. Now I want the safety and love found in his outstretched arms.

TRUST

I trust your promises, Oh Lord
Keep my spirit calm.
Remind me you are my strong tower
I can run into the tower and be safe.
Let your love radiate around me
Always remind me I am your child
And I am safe.

I talk to God some days now. I know he has forgiven me for breaking our friendship. I struggle with what to say to my friend. My friend is very patient.

He listens and I hear his voice.

20
FINDING LIFE AGAIN

How did I find life again? At first I thought this was an interesting question but one I had no answer for.

In time, with much reflection, this is my attempt to share what finding life again became for me. It became seeing old things like emotions, our natural surroundings, our relationships and life events with a totally refreshed and vibrant outlook; as if seeing life for the first time.

I liken it to being a baby and relearning how to do everything again. There were lots of "firsts" to experience.

Those firsts included laughter, jokes, humor. Lunch with friends. Firsts were difficult initially. It meant stretching outside my comfort zone of hiding from life. I had fun shopping again. I was able to go out to dinner and relax, enjoy the moment. I enjoyed short day visits even though they caused anxiety. The friendly visits and all the "new" things that I used to do without thinking were about me finding life again.

To me it means valuing the journey to be traveled and to embracing the changes that come with the journey.

I see this part of my journey as a time for joyous celebration when I am at my peak. The peaks are wonderful times and places, but I need to remember when I step into a valley that I will move through this part of my journey too. For that matter, the valleys are not as deep as they once were.

Finding life again for me is a time not to be caught up in all the trappings around me and become self absorbed. I see life as reaching out and becoming an encourager to those around me. Finding life means living an outward journey that leads me to meet new people, do new things, and dream big dreams. I took a knitting class and met new people. I hope to eventually join a knitting club to sit, swap stories and of course knit.

I began to play the dulcimer a beautiful instrument I first heard while living in Tennessee two decades ago.

I volunteer one day a week at a nursing home. This has helped me focus on another person's journey through life. My big dream now is to work someday in a university setting. This is a really big dream. It is great to have big dreams, and some dreams really do come true.

Finding life again means looking for the light, not the dark in the world. As I look for this light I look for it in myself, my spouse, my family, my friends and my natural surroundings.

Finding life again is like seeing life through a stained glass window. I see its exquisite, color and find the color that is me. Everyone has a different color and together with everyone having their own color and shining forth you find a way to live life with everyone you love and with everyone you meet on your journey.

Finding life again means I live more simply now. My life is not cluttered with to-do lists. Every event is not an emergency. There is a time to relax, reflect and enjoy life. There is time for friends. There is time to learn new things in my world.

So this is my story.

I hope you have a better understanding of where one person's journey with mental illness had her travel a path that had many twists and turns and the end result is that I found life again. The journey continues.

Psychologist and author Leo Buscaglia, once wrote, "I still get wildly enthusiastic about little things... I play with leaves. I skip down the street and run against the wind! "

This is me. Simply.

One day me be fine.

ONE DAY ME BE FINE

ABOUT THE AUTHOR

Susan K. Brown is a former elementary school teacher and university administrator who earned her education degree from The Ohio State University and her master's degree in reading education from The University of Tennessee. She has taught in both private and public schools. Her entrepreneurial spirit has led to work in the corporate world and to owning her own business. Susan is a lover of all things beautiful and lovely. With her husband she has made her home in Ohio, Tennessee, Indiana, and Pennsylvania.